T0063479

SAVED,
SINGLE, *and*
SATISFIED

VICKIE BLAKENEY MITCHELL

Order this book online at www.trafford.com
or email orders@trafford.com

Most Trafford titles are also available at major online book retailers.

All scriptures were cited from the Holy Bible New King James Version.
© Thomas Nelson Inc. 1982, unless otherwise indicated by KJV (King James Version)
KJV reference Bible © Zondervan 1994

Printed in the United States of America.

ISBN: 978-1-4907-3379-1 (sc)
ISBN: 978-1-4907-3381-4 (hc)
ISBN: 978-1-4907-3380-7 (e)

Library of Congress Control Number: 2014907024

Trafford rev. 04/14/2014

 www.trafford.com

North America & international
toll-free: 1 888 232 4444 (USA & Canada)
fax: 812 355 4082

I would like to give thanks to my Lord and Savior for giving me the inspiration to write this book. I dedicate it to my husband, Curtis, and son, Kristian. Thank you both for allowing me the opportunity to spend the time necessary to see it to completion. Also, I give thanks to my mother, Naomi and all other family members, coworkers, church members, and friends for your support and feedback. I sincerely thank each and every one of you.

Vickie Blakeney Mitchell

CONTENTS

PREFACE

In 2004, while working as a cytotechnologist, I struggled with being single and living a life in Christ. But through faith, and studying and living the Word of Christ, I was able to understand and endure my current state. In this profession, you screen slides all day with a microscope, leaving me with plenty of time to listen to the Bible on CDs. I was teaching Bible study to teenagers and was a faithful member of my church and community. One day, I expressed my personal struggle with being a Christian single and trying to live a Christian lifestyle to a coworker. I further informed her of how gaining a closer relationship with Christ, vowing to live according to his Word, and trusting and believing that he will send me my husband helped the struggle and, eventually, gave me peace, patience, and understanding of the reason for waiting on him to send the proper mate. She asked if I would come to her church and speak to the Singles' Ministry Sunday School class about my experience and give some encouragement to those in a similar circumstance. I was single, a divorced mother striving to live a Christian lifestyle.

After accepting the invitation, I asked the Lord to give me a message, an encouraging word to give to those in my situation, and he gave me "Saved, single, and satisfied." One of the deacons from my church accompanied me that day and reported back to my pastor about the message and the response. I was then asked to speak to my congregation with the same message.

For many years afterward, I would allow individuals the opportunity to read a copy of it, and I always get the same response, "You need to tell this message to all singles. You need to put it in a book." I held on to the message for years, with it tucked safely away in a folder. The Holy Spirit constantly whispered in my ear, "Tell my message. Feed my sheep." But I did not have the platform by which to tell the message.

Years later, I was asked to facilitate a class at a Singles' Summit, and I used this message. The door was opened, and the platform emerged. I later gave the same message at a Women's Conference, and again, I got the same response, "People need to hear this message."

INTRODUCTION

Do you find yourself asking the all-too-familiar question, "Why am I still single?" Many unmarried believers of Christ and nonbelievers as well ask this perplexing question. They find themselves pondering what it is that their married counterparts possess that they are lacking.

In the twenty-first century, we have encountered a population of people that is growing at an astronomical rate. This population is termed as "singles" and defined as those individuals that have never been married, those that were married and now divorced, those that are widowed, and those that are married but separated and living as a single person. This population is growing constantly because of a number of variables. Individuals are more career driven today than ever before and, therefore, getting married at later stages of life. Also, there is an increase in divorce rate. Single Christians are also encountering individuals with commitment issues and less opportunity to be evenly yoked. Whatever the reasons may be in today's society, this population continues to encounter their own individual set of circumstances, revelations, and challenges, including church attendance, finances, ministry participation, salvation, dating, relationships, and living a Christian lifestyle.

Due to the "anything goes" mentality of a vastly large denomination of people today, single Christians are finding it more and more difficult to lean not unto their own understanding and wait upon the Lord for direction. Single Christians are struggling to live a lifestyle that the scripture has instructed, which will be rewarded with abundance, prosperity, and eternal life. Single unbelievers as well as believers are feeling the sense of loneliness and isolation from their married counterparts. They start falling victim to the old cliché "My biological clock is ticking" and being reminded that, historically, women were married by a certain age or they were referred to as an old maid. Many singles, especially women, feel the desire to be married or "involved," which thereby causes a sense of desperation, resulting in poor choices and, ultimately, being left with dealing with the consequences.

Single Christians, as well as the unbelievers, find themselves turning to the clubs, parties, and online matchmaking in order to find the mate that they desire, ultimately believing that these relationships will turn into the answer to their quest. Salvation, purging and purification, dating, relationships, growing in faith, and the role of the man and woman are all areas that many single Christians and unbelievers question. Even after gaining salvation, they continue to struggle with being a single Christian, trying to live a Christian lifestyle and being completely satisfied with their current state of singleness.

Many of us have sinned and fallen short of his glory at some point in our lives. This book is in no way meant to be judgmental; it is for the purpose of bringing awareness to those that find themselves in a state of singleness and desire to know the requirements for living a Christian lifestyle. *Saved, Single, and Satisfied* will help empower singles to gain and understand the meaning of salvation, how to purge and purify themselves, and how to seek a new heart. It will help singles grow in their faith, avoid the pitfalls of dating, and know how to maintain or discontinue relationships. It will also help singles understand the biblical role of a man and a woman and to ultimately be satisfied with themselves and with being single.

THE MESSAGE

Saved, Single, and Satisfied

I WANT TO BRIEFLY TELL YOU why I am passionate in the ministry of singles. I suffered through singleness for many years before getting married and divorced. The reason why I suffered was because I didn't know then what I know now. I will not spend a lot of time discussing the issue of my failed marriage. I learned my lesson from it, and I am now moving forward, not dwelling in the past. I used to spend a lot of time dwelling on it and blaming my ex-husband for everything that went wrong. Sometimes I felt as if I would go crazy, allowing him to control my emotions. I was very bitter. It wasn't until I began to study the Word of Christ and trying to live according to his Word that I finally realized I was the one to blame.

I have been a Christian for as long as I can remember. I grew up in church, and as an adult, I attended Bible study and prayer meetings. At that time, I thought I was doing halfway right. But I still did what I wanted to do (what the flesh wanted to do). I read the Word, but I really wasn't living the Word, and that's a big difference. You know the saying "Playing church"—what a lot of Christians do today.

When I was single the first time, I was so tired of meeting the same old type of people. Attracting married men, men that didn't want a committed relationship, and you know— let me be real for a minute—the kind that just wanted to, as they call it, hit it. Sometimes I thought I had a big sign on my forehead, "desperate" in neon lights. People thought I had such a perfect life, thought I had it going on. Single, had by own house, my own car, and a good job. But what they didn't realize was, I was so lonely. I cried a lot, and that feeling of loneliness caused me to make some bad decisions. My life was empty. Now that I look back on it, I understand why. Although I called myself a Christian, I didn't truly have the Spirit of Christ in my life. I was not living a Christian lifestyle.

So when an old boyfriend and I got back together and he asked me to marry him, I jumped at the opportunity. I just wanted to be married. Big mistake! There is a lot more to marriage than just wanting to be married. My decision was also made without God. That's where so many of us go wrong; we jump to what the flesh wants to do instead of seeking what God wants us to do, which will come from not having a relationship with him.

The signs were there; I was making a mistake but chose not to listen. I was involved in an accident on the way to the wedding that detained almost half of the guests and causing the wedding to start very late. That's why I say that looking back, it was my fault; the signs were there. If we develop a relationship with the Lord and seek his advice, then he will reveal things to us that will prevent some of our pitfalls.

We need to first realize the meaning of true salvation and how to receive it. Then we need to understand our singleness and how to purge and purify ourselves so we can seek a life in Christ, be led by the Holy Spirit, and acknowledge that just because we are single, it does not mean we are lonely or alone.

Finally, we have to be satisfied with ourselves and know that God has a reason for the state that we are currently in.

As singles, the first thing you need to do is to seek ye first the kingdom of heaven. You have to choose to have a life with Christ or a life without Christ; it's as simple as that. It's not like ordering from Burger King, where you have all those choices. Imagine, you're at Burger King, uh! Then when you finally make a choice, you can even have it your way. Put what you want on your sandwich. Well, unlike Burger King, this is a simple choice, with or without, and you can't have it both ways. It's either one or the other. To be a true Christian seeking salvation, you cannot straddle the fence. You cannot continue to live in the world and want to be saved at the same time.

Secondly, we then have to repent for our sins and ask the Lord to forgive us and believe Romans 10:9, "If you confess with your mouth the Lord Jesus and believe in your heart that God has raised Him from the dead, you will be saved." That sounds pretty easy, huh? But it doesn't stop there; there's a lot of work to do.

Now remember, I had a lot of bitterness from my marriage. Ephesians 4:31 reads, "Let all bitterness, wrath, anger, clamor, and evil speaking be put away from you, with all malice." It took me a long time to submit to this command. But with the help of the Lord, all things are possible. And don't think it happens overnight, because it doesn't.

Bitterness is destructive inside your body. It tears up your insides and hurts no one but you. So you have to ask the Lord for forgiveness and let it go. If we take a look at all that we do in our lives that are sins against the Lord and he will still forgive us, we need to be able to get rid of the bitterness, forgive others, and move on. You cannot successfully move from one relationship to another holding bitterness from a past relationship. You cannot have a healthy relationship harboring bitterness from the past. We have to remember the scripture "These things I command you that you love one another" (John 15:17). The Lord said, "How are you going to love me whom you haven't seen if you can't even love your brother whom you have seen?"

Thirdly, we have to allow the Lord to purge and purify us in order to live by his will. *Purge* is to get rid of anything in the body or the flesh that causes us to sin. *Purify* is to make clean, and only the Lord can do that. It takes the blood of Jesus to make us clean. Psalm 51:2 reads, "Wash me thoroughly from mine iniquity, and cleanse me from my sin." Psalm 51:10 reads, "Create in me a clean heart, O God; and renew a steadfast spirit within me." Like David, we have to ask him to cleanse us and then ask for a new heart and a new spirit. We know "the heart is deceitful above all things, and desperately wicked" (Jeremiah 17:9). The old heart wants the flesh to be happy. And did you know that it is the heart that determines whether or not you enter the kingdom?

Do you remember the story of Achan in the seventh chapter of Joshua? The Lord instructed Joshua and the Israelites to attack the city of Ai. He would deliver the city into their hands, but he instructed them to remember to destroy everything and to keep away from the devoted things to avoid destruction to themselves. Those devoted things were pagan gods and other things that the people worshipped instead of God. Israel was not able, however, to defeat its enemy as the Lord promised. Achan, acting with a deceitful heart, coveted some of the things he saw, so he took the plunder, a robe from Babylonia, silver, and gold. Whoever said, "One bad apple doesn't spoil the whole bunch"?

The Lord instructed Joshua to purge Achan from the city because of his disobedience. Achan and his entire family were stoned to death. After the command was fulfilled, Joshua and the Israelites continued to be blessed by the Lord. For us, the devoted things may be people, sexual desire, fornication, drinking, coveting, and anything that comes between you and the Lord. We are to keep away from these things. "How much more shall the blood of Christ, who through the eternal Spirit offered Himself without spot to God, purge your conscience from dead works to serve the living God" (Hebrews 9:14 KJV). You must purge anything that is causing you not to have a relationship with God. Like Joshua with Achan, you must rid your body of all things that is causing you not to be blessed.

Now we need to talk about some things that people usually do not discuss in a church setting. But that is an issue we need to overcome because the world is very quick to teach us contrary to what we need to be taught as Christians. Amen!

First, I want to tell you that some of us like to avoid certain scriptures because they step on too many toes. They may even sound hypercritical. This is why a lot of ministers and pastors may not even preach or teach on certain issues. But I had to think about the definition of a hypocrite. If you once did a particular thing and you know that it was not of the will of God, and you no longer do it. You are not a hypocrite when you try to help others learn from your mistake. Other people can learn from our testimony. I will not point a finger at you without including myself. I still go through a lot of the struggles that you are going through as singles, but I thank God I am not where I used to be. So I am in the trenches with you. If this two-edge sword cuts, then that is a good thing because if it doesn't cut you and you can't say, "Ouch," you don't have the conscience to realize the faults in your own life. If the sword cuts, you will heal and you can receive salvation, the kingdom of heaven, and eternal life. But it has to hurt first.

"Or do you not know that your body is the temple of the Holy Spirit who is in you, whom you have from God, and you are not your own?" (1 Corinthians 6:19). Your body doesn't even belong to you. Do you know that when you are living in the world, you possess evil spirits that make you do whatever is pleasing to the flesh? So in sexual relationships, when you join your body with another person, you are merging your spirit with their spirit. This is why the Word tells us to wait until marriage. Every time we engage in fornication, we take on that person's spirit. That's why another person can have control over you emotionally, physically, and mentally. Now think of all the spirits you may have mixed with yours. Do I need to give you a moment to count? Now all these spirits, mixed with any other sins, will cause the temple not to be clean. When your spirit is not clean, you will attract unclean spirits. And the Holy Spirit will definitely not dwell in a dirty house. This is why we keep attracting unclean spirits. This includes people that don't want a committed relationship, people who don't want to respect your desire to wait until marriage, and unsaved people who have no desire whatsoever in seeking salvation.

You may be attracting men that don't want to work; there are a lot of those out there now. They are just looking for a sugar mama. This is why we have to purge and purify ourselves by asking the Lord to wash us clean. You will continue to attract the wrong kind of people if you don't ask the Lord to cleanse you. It's all over your body, and that's the image that comes out. Again, we have to remember that our bodies do not belong to us; we are bought and paid for by the blood of Jesus.

Cleaning up our lives without filling it with God's Word leaves plenty of room for Satan to enter. So ridding our lives of sin is just the first step. We must also take the second step in filling our lives with God's Word and the Holy Spirit. Unfilled and complacent people are easy targets for Satan. It's like digging a hole and not filling it back up with dirt; when left unattended, someone can easily fall into it. "When an unclean spirit goes out of a man, he goes through dry places, seeking rest, and finds none. Then he says, 'I will return to my house from which I came.' And when he comes, he finds it empty, swept, and put in order. Then he goes and takes with him seven other spirits more wicked than himself, and they enter and dwell there; and the last state of that man is worse than the first. So shall it also be with this wicked generation" (Matthew 12:43-45).

This is why, after cleansing, you have to fill your life with God's Word. When those evil spirits try to come back, you want them to flee from you. If you are not then living by the Word, they will set up shop again, and remember, the scripture said they bring friends, "seven other spirits more wicked than himself." This is why you see a person that has tried to give up drugs, smoking, or sex, and when they don't fill their life with the Word, the spirits come back, and the person may start doing things worse than before, like fighting or very bold sexual behaviors.

Today, we are drowning in a sea of impurity. Everywhere we look, we find temptation to lead impure lives. We constantly see it on TV, videos, etc. So you may ask the question, "How do we stay pure in a filthy environment?" We cannot do this on our own. We must have strength more powerful than the tempting influences around us. So how do we find the strength and the wisdom? By reading God's Word and doing what he tells us to do.

When I finally decided to make a change in my life, I said, "Okay, Lord, I submit myself to you. I will do the best that I can to live by your Word." I gave up ungodly behaviors, got rid of the bitterness, and started trusting in the Lord. That's when I knew that I started being led by the Holy Spirit. He started talking to me, leading and guiding me to make the right decisions. I knew that he was in my heart. When you allow the Holy Spirit to lead you, you'll find that you have no desire to do the things you used to do. The Holy Spirit has the power of conviction. If you slip and do something that's not of the will of God, the power of conviction will break you down.

Some of you may have heard of the vow of purity. Some churches will have a monthlong training session of the vow of purity and its meaning. Basically, it means after submitting to Christ, you take a vow to be married to him and remain pure until you are earthly married. So I decided I would take my own vow of purity. Now remember, I said that everything doesn't happen overnight. Well, here I go again giving into the fleshly desire, and man, I cried like a baby afterward. The power of conviction broke me down. I felt the disappointment of the Lord; it was so heavy on my heart, and I did not want to feel that way again.

Let's stay on the subject of fornication and sexual desire for a moment because if you are honest with yourself, you will realize that this is the biggest area that causes a separation between single people and the Lord. "Blessed is the man who endures temptation; for when he has been approved, he will receive the crown of life which the Lord has promised to those who love Him" (James 1:12). So if we love the Lord, he will help us resist temptations of the flesh, and as promised, we will receive the crown of life. "Therefore submit to God. Resist the devil and he will flee from you" (James 4:7). Don't be controlled by the flesh. It's a choice to do or not to do.

I know sometimes you want a man's arms around you. I know; I have been there. When I was in the world, the sex was not the desire. It was the feeling of being loved and having a man's arms around me; I could do without the sex. I wanted the feeling of being safe and secure. But you know what I found out? The Lord and Savior Jesus Christ will give you that same feeling. So don't say that you are lonely, because the Lord said, "I will be with you always." What man or woman can make that promise?

Let me pause and give you an illustration. How many of you have children? Do you get tired of your children disobeying you, and you have to keep telling them the same thing over and over again? Well, the Lord feels the same way about us. He gives us the commands, and we continue to do what we want to do over and over again. For example, you tell your children to stay away from the stove so they will not get burned. They will continue to play around the stove until they actually get burned. The Lord gives us the commands, and we disobey. He tells us if we don't repent, we die! We expect a child to obey, but we don't. Let me give you another example; your child gets in the cookie jar after being told not to touch the cookies. Mother asks, "Have you been in the cookie jar?" Child responds, "No." The evidence is all over their face. Likewise, you go out on Saturday night, party, and have a good time jamming to Ja Rule, Master P, and 50 Cent. You do everything under the sun that you want to do and come to church on Sunday, praising the Lord, shouting, "Amen, preach it, Pastor!" Who do you think you are fooling? Maybe the people, but the Lord can see the evidence; it's all over you. Been there, done that.

Remember, the body is the temple. If you are sleeping with a man and letting him violate your temple, you are missing out on your blessings by not living by the will of

God. So ask yourself, "Why? Why am I subjecting myself to damnation, and when I need that man to really be there for me, where is he?" So again, why are you letting someone make you miss out on your blessings? It took me many years to understand this concept, but thank you, Jesus, I finally got it. "I was blind but now I see." "Marriage is honourable in all, and the bed undefiled: but whoremongers and adulterers, God will judge" (Hebrews 13:4 KJV). Ouch! Do I need to explain this scripture? Like I said, we try to skirt around certain scriptures. It's time to wake up and smell the coffee burning and be real about the Word. Do you think I liked being referred to as a whoremonger? Let's see, not married, having sexual relations—whoremonger. Ouch! Like my son says, dah! This sword hurts, but don't get mad at me. I didn't write the scripture. It hurts me too! So wait until marriage.

I briefly want to mention homosexuality and lesbianism since this is a worldly act that is becoming so popular. If we study the second chapter of Genesis, we will understand the Lord's formation of the family. The Lord saw that Adam needed a helpmeet, meaning someone best suitable for him. The Lord then created Eve for Adam from one of his ribs. In the scriptures, the Lord was very straightforward about fornication and homosexuality. He destroyed the entire cities of Sodom and Gomorrah with fire and brimstone because of homosexuality and indecent sexual activity. It seems to be happening all over again. We have public officials, pastors, movie stars, and laypeople all having indecent sexual behaviors and are being exposed on national news daily.

Let me briefly say this. We have to get back to the original formation of the family. What we have done throughout the years have really caused an impact on the lives of our children. Each generation is losing more and more of the biblical perception of family. We are raising our children in single-parent homes, getting divorces at the drop of a hat, and constantly satisfying the flesh. I am guilty myself. It has caused a great impact on our children; we are hurting them and teaching them that family is not important. We, as a nation, have to turn this thing around. We have to explain to our children that we and our parents and grandparents made mistakes, but the Holy Bible tells the formation of a family. We have to teach them what is right and start showing them by example. I myself made this mistake, being tired of being single and deciding to handle it myself and not wait on God. I look at what problems it causes my son. I never wanted to be a divorced parent. It hurts when my child wants his father to pick him up from school because he sees his classmates' fathers picking them up. It hurts when his father missed some of his soccer games or his plays at school. This is what happens when we try to do God's work. Our children suffer!

I used to listen to a female talk show host and psychotherapist on the radio. She made an interesting statement one day that really made an impact on me. She said, "Prostitutes have more sense than some of us. At least they charge two hundred fifty dollars a pop. We give it away!" This was an eye-opener for me, because, come on now, if we are not married and sleeping with a man, we are, in essence, giving it away. Why buy the software when you can download it free? We are going to be real because, I say again, we are living in our last days, and we have to stop skirting around certain issues and just get to the point.

So the question becomes, "How do I stop the sexual desires?" Go to the Lord; remember, nothing is too hard for God. Submit to his will. Repent and ask for forgiveness. Let the Lord cleanse and purify you. Then you have to make an inventory of what you do throughout your day. For me, I had to get rid of everything in my house that remotely reminded me of the act. I bagged it all up and set it out on the curb for garbage pickup. Some things for you may be ex-rated videos, as well as those on TV. Tell the truth, you look at LL Cool J on his video and you all know you lose your mind. Also, all the stuff that is shown on television and movies may not be suitable. Stop watching late-night cable, etc., stop clubbing, and sometimes you have to let some of those friends go.

Dating is another big issue. You have to be careful with this. Stop putting yourself in certain situations. If you are at a man's house and your flesh gets weak, get your butt out of there. Don't expect God to help you if you keep putting yourself in these situations.

When you accept Christ in your life, your life starts transforming because you are seeking the Father in the kingdom of heaven. In the twentieth chapter of John, Mary Magdalene waited for Jesus by the sepulcher, weeping. She turned around and saw Jesus standing. When she finally realized that it was Jesus, she called out to him, "Master." Jesus said to her, "Touch me not for I am not yet ascended to my Father." When you seek salvation, you are ascending into another part of your life. If anyone, man or woman, gets in your way, say, "Touch me not. [Give them the hand.] Don't touch me, don't put your lips on me, back up." Don't let anyone or anything interfere with your ascension to the Father.

Getting back to that fleshly feeling of loneliness—make sure Jesus Christ is in your heart, your spirit, and your mind, so you are not lonely. Avoid making crazy decisions that we make in the heat of being lonely and desperate.

You all know what a maintenance man is, right? I'm not talking about someone that will fix the boards on your house either. Do not call on a maintenance man! You can call on Jesus in the midnight hour if you think you are alone. But remember, with Jesus, you are never alone! I know you get weak sometimes. But remember, "Fear not, for I am with you; be not dismayed, for I am your God. I will strengthen you, Yes, I will help you, I will uphold you with My righteous right hand" (Isaiah 41:10). So don't worry about being alone. The Lord said, "I will never leave you nor forsake you" (Joshua 1:5). So call on him.

Finally, we need to be content with being single. We need to realize that the Lord is working on us right now. You have to be satisfied and content being an individual in Christ before you are ready to share a life with someone else. A lot of us are not ready spiritually to be married. For example, when you get married, ladies, you then have to realize that you have a *head*! Did you hear what I said? If you are not ready to accept that the man is head of the household, you are not ready for that commitment. Men, if you want to continue to be a mama's boy, don't get married. If you keep letting Mama or Daddy take care of you, how do you think you are ready to be the head of a household and take care of a family? If you are not ready to take on the responsibility of being the head, don't get married; stay single. Women, if you can't clean your house or apartments now, if you can't cook, and if you can't be responsible, how do you think you are going to take care of the needs of a family? Children are not rag dolls; you cannot put them down, drop them off, and pick them up when you want to.

When you get married, your family comes second only to God. Right now, you can pay your bills when you want to. You can write a check when you feel like it, and the money you make is yours. All of these things change when you get married. Getting married is not just for convenience; it is a spiritual commitment!

Singles, this is the perfect time of your life to work on yourself and develop a better relationship with the Lord. He can direct your path and mold you into the person that he wants you to be so you can be ready when he sends you your spouse. The Lord wants us to continue to be molded in his own image. So while he is over here preparing you, he is also over there molding and perfecting your mate. Now, women, you have to realize there are only a few men that are allowing the Lord to work with them. So if you are not molded and seeking a life in Christ, do you think he is going to give you one of the few so you can mess him up? Come on now. Men, the same goes for you.

(This is very important.) Don't get caught up in what material things a person may have. Use this time to buy your own house, your own car, and your own clothes. When you allow a man to do these things for you, you get caught up and you cannot adequately judge his character. Anything that you have that a man bought, give it back so you have no ties and no obligations to him.

Women, stop looking for a husband. The scripture does not say, "She who findeth a husband," but "He who finds a wife finds a good thing, And obtains favor from the Lord" (Proverbs 18:22). Stop complaining about not being married and not having a relationship. Stop asking the Lord, "Please send me someone." Get your house in order. Work on your finances, your children, your spirit, and any other aspect of your life that may need some attention. Remember when Moses was leading the Israelites out of Egypt? They were complaining about eating manna; they were not content. They were so tired of eating manna. They kept asking for meat. To teach them a lesson, God gave them so much meat that it was coming out of their nostrils. So God knows your heart. Stop complaining before he sends you so many men that you get confused and you get totally tripped up. The Lord has a way of punishing his children when he wants to teach us to live by his command.

In closing, I want to leave you with this, "And I will give you the keys of the kingdom of heaven, and whatever you bind on earth will be bound in heaven, and whatever you loose on earth will be loosed in heaven" (Matthew 16:19). Don't let being single bound you up. Use it to lift you up. Spend time in the Word of Christ. Use it to regain your life. Cleanse your spirit. Let the Holy Spirit come in and dwell in your temple. Be a diamond in the rough. The Lord knows your potential; he sees what's on the inside, even when the world sees only what's on the outside. When a diamond is found, it looks all roughed up; it looks like a piece of charcoal, but the miner knows what's on the inside. When you are living in the world, like the ugly coal, your mother may want to give up and throw you away or your daddy may want to give up on you. But like the miner, God knows what's on the inside. If you come to him and submit to his will and start studying the Word, the Word then becomes the chisel, and he will chisel away the ugly outside. The Lord throws that ugly outside away, not back at you. You know those things that you did while you were in the world that people don't let you forget. As long as you stay in the Word, he continues to chisel, and soon, the perfect diamond is exposed for the entire world to see. So for now, seek salvation, be single, and be satisfied.

CHAPTER 1

Salvation

That if you confess with your mouth the Lord Jesus and believe in your heart that God has raised Him from the dead, you will be saved.

—Romans 10:9

WHAT MUST I DO TO be saved? Salvation is attained only through faith in Christ. In order to receive salvation, one must believe in your heart and then confess with your mouth that Jesus is Lord and he has risen from the dead, and then you will be saved. The Lord gave his only Son to be sacrificed on the cross so that we can be free from sin and from Satan's control. Salvation grants us freedom from the darkness of Satan's dominion, and he no longer has any power over us. It is through God's grace that he has delivered us and brought us into the light of his kingdom. We no longer have to live in bondage; we have been set free.

Salvation cannot be earned because it is a gift from God and available to all that desire it. It cannot be purchased and cannot be taken away. Salvation is by God's grace. Receiving salvation means to turn from our sins and is a desire to have

1

a relationship with God. Those that receive salvation become God's children, united with him, and heirs to his throne.

In the seventh chapter of Luke, we are reminded of how a sinful woman anointed Jesus' feet. Simon the Pharisee asked Jesus to have dinner with him. Jesus went to the Pharisee's house and reclined at the table. When an uninvited woman from the town that lived a sinful life learned that Jesus was eating at the Pharisee's house, she brought an alabaster jar of perfume and stood at Jesus' feet, weeping. She began wetting Jesus' feet with her tears, wiped them with her hair, kissed them, and poured the perfumed on them. Unlike the Pharisee that did not offer Jesus any water for his feet, she was forgiven of her sins. Jesus told the woman she was saved by her faith and to go in peace.

Jesus loves us, and through salvation, no matter how many times we sin, he will always be there. We can repent and ask for forgiveness. He said he will never leave us or forsake us (Hebrews 13:5). Even at times in our lives when we have turned away from him, he was still there. David stated, "If I ascend into heaven, You are there; If I make my bed in hell, behold, You are there" (Psalm 139:8)

THE WORD

Colossians 1:13-14

> He has delivered us from the power of darkness and conveyed us into the kingdom of the Son of His love, in whom we have redemption through His blood, the forgiveness of sins.

John 1:12-13

But as many as received Him, to them He gave the right to become children of God, to those who believe in His name: who were born, not of blood, nor of the will of the flesh, nor of the will of man, but of God.

Romans 6:1-4

What shall we say then? Shall we continue in sin that grace may abound? Certainly not! How shall we who died to sin live any longer in it? Or do you not know that as many of us as were baptized into Christ Jesus were baptized into His death? Therefore we were buried with Him through baptism into death, that just as Christ was raised from the dead by the glory of the Father, even so we also should walk in newness of life.

Ephesians 2:1-3

And you He made alive, who were dead in trespasses and sins, in which you once walked according to the course of this world, according to the prince of the power of the air, the spirit who now works in the sons of disobedience, among whom also we all once conducted ourselves in the lusts of our flesh, fulfilling the desires of the flesh and of the mind, and were by nature children of wrath, just as the others.

John 10:9-10

> I am the door. If anyone enters by Me, he will be saved, and will go in and out and find pasture. The thief does not come except to steal, and to kill, and to destroy. I have come that they may have life, and that they may have it more abundantly.

John 3:16

> For God so loved the world that He gave His only begotten Son, that whoever believes in Him should not perish but have everlasting life.

SISTA TO SISTA

Go in peace, my sista! Jesus died so that you no longer have to be controlled by your human nature. You no longer have to live in darkness under Satan's dominion. If you have faith and believe in your heart and confess with your mouth that Jesus is Lord and he has risen from the dead, then you are saved. You can go to God through Jesus and ask for forgiveness when you sin. He is a loving God, and he wants the best for you, which is life in his eternal kingdom.

When you realize that you have sinned, repent and ask God for forgiveness. He is a loving God and will welcome us back into his arms of protection. We are saved through his grace, and absolutely no one can take that away.

DISCUSSION

_____

_____

_____

_____

_____

_____

_____

_____

_____

_____

_____

_____

_____

_____

_____

_____

_____

_____

_____

_____

_____

_____

_____

_____

_____

_____

_____

_____

_____

_____

CHAPTER 2

Purge and Purify

Therefore, having these promises, beloved, let us cleanse ourselves from all filthiness of the flesh and spirit, perfecting holiness in the fear of God.
—2 Corinthians 7:1

Create in me a clean heart, O God; and renew a right spirit within me.
—Psalm 51:10 KJV

In today's society, we are living in a sea of impurity with endless temptations to lead impure lives. We are constantly reminded of the wickedness of the environment around us. In the media, we have music videos that are sexually explicit, and professional athletes, movie stars, and politicians with multiple partners, resulting in countless children out of wedlock. Illegal drugs are available on every corner, and women are being exploiting day in and day out.

The media continues to glamorize what is contradictory to biblical teaching; that one should remain pure until marriage and thou shalt not commit adultery are among a few. Many would think or believe that purity is a thing of the past, believing that this way of thinking is old-fashioned and outdated. However, the Lord requires purity for a number of reasons, including not defiling the body, avoiding diseases, and not causing separation between us and God.

"Or do you not know that your body is the temple of the Holy Spirit who is in you, whom you have from God, and you are not your own?" (1 Corinthians 6:19). Your body doesn't even belong to you. Do you know that when you are living in the world, you possess evil spirits that make you do whatever is pleasing to the flesh? So in sexual relationships, when you join your body with another person, you are merging your spirit with their spirit. This is why the Word tells us to wait until marriage. Every time we engage in fornication, we take on that person's spirit. That's why another person can have control over your emotions, physically and mentally.

When your spirit is not clean, you will attract unclean spirits. This include people that don't want a committed relationship, people who don't want to respect your desire to wait until marriage, and unsaved people who have no desire whatsoever in seeking salvation. This is why we have to purge and purify ourselves by asking the Lord to wash us clean. You will continue to attract the wrong kind of people if you don't ask the Lord to cleanse you. It's all over your body, and that's the image that comes out. Again, we have to remember that our bodies do not belong to us; we are bought and paid for by the blood of Jesus.

So you may ask the question, "How do we stay pure in a filthy environment?" We cannot do this on our own. We must have strength more powerful than the tempting influences around us. So how do we find the strength and the wisdom? By reading God's Word and doing what he tells us to do.

Just as the Corinthians were encouraged to have nothing to do with paganism, we too have to break away from the world and our past and give ourselves completely to God (2 Corinthians 7:1). We have to allow the Lord to purge and purify us in order to live by his will. *Purge* is to get rid of anything in the body or the flesh that causes us to sin. *Purify* is to make clean. It takes the blood of Jesus to make us clean. Like David, we have to ask him to cleanse us and then ask for a new heart and a new spirit because we know "the heart is deceitful above all things and desperately wicked" (Jeremiah 17:9). The old heart wants the flesh to be happy. Take the vow of purity, a vow to be married to him, and remain pure until you are earthly married. Let go of all bitterness and strife from past relationships.

Just as the Lord promised to Solomon, "If my people, which are called by my name, shall humble themselves, and pray, and seek my face, and turn from their wicked ways; then will I hear from heaven, and will forgive their sin, and will heal their land" (2 Chronicles 7:14). Here we have four conditions: (1) we must humble ourselves, (2) we must pray, (3) we must seek his face, and (4) we must turn from wicked ways (sin). These are the conditions for sin to be forgiven and for healing to take place.

THE WORD

Psalm 51:2

> Wash me thoroughly from my iniquity, and cleanse me from my sin.

1 John 2:16-17

> For all that is in the world—the lust of the flesh, the lust of the eyes, and the pride of life—is not

of the Father but is of the world. And the world is passing away, and the lust of it; but he who does the will of God abides forever.

1 Thessalonians 4:3-7

For this is the will of God, your sanctification: that you should abstain from sexual immorality; that each of you should know how to possess his own vessel in sanctification and honor, not in passion of lust, like the Gentiles who do not know God; that no one should take advantage of and defraud his brother in this matter, because the Lord is the avenger of all such, as we also forewarned you and testified. For God did not call us to uncleanness, but in holiness.

Matthew 15:19-20

For out of the heart proceed evil thoughts, murders, adulteries, fornications, thefts, false witness, blasphemies. These are the things which defile a man, but to eat with unwashed hands does not defile a man.

1 Corinthians 6:19-20

Or do you not know that your body is the temple of the Holy Spirit who is in you, whom you have from God, and you are not your own? For you were bought at a price; therefore glorify God in your body and in your spirit, which are God's.

Jeremiah 3:14

"Return, O backsliding children," says the Lord; "for I am married to you. I will take you, one from a city and two from a family, and I will bring you to Zion."

2 Chronicles 7:14

If My people who are called by My name will humble themselves, and pray and seek My face, and turn from their wicked ways, then I will hear from heaven, and will forgive their sin and heal their land.

SISTA TO SISTA

Sista, stop allowing men to defile your temple. Repent for past sins of sexual behavior, and ask the Lord for help to guard your thoughts and actions against lust and premarital sex. Stay out of situations that would cause your flesh to get weak and fall into temptation. Continue to pray for strength and call upon the Lord when the flesh is weakened. Schedule more opportunities for you to interact with small groups of people with similar interest, and engage your thoughts and actions into other avenues. Remember, he is a loving God and is waiting with his arms stretched wide for you to return to him.

DISCUSSION

CHAPTER 3

Growing in Christ

Therefore, laying aside all malice, all deceit, hypocrisy, envy, and all evil speaking, as newborn babes, desire the pure milk of the word that you may grow thereby, if indeed you have tasted that the Lord is gracious.

—1 Peter 2:1-3

I AM SAVED, I AM SAVED, I am saved! Now what? After you receive salvation, you become a new creature, and a conversion should take place. You are, at that point, a new convert. You will then receive the Holy Spirit, and you are considered born again. In the ninth chapter of Acts, we find Saul's conversion. Saul, being led by his Jewish beliefs, led a campaign to persecute all who believed in Christ. He believed that Jesus had died and was buried in a Judean grave, and there he remained. As he traveled to Damascus in pursuit of Christians, he was confronted by the living Christ. There was a light that shone around him from heaven, which caused Saul to fall to the ground. Saul heard the voice of Christ, saying, "Saul, Saul, why persecutes thou me?" Saul then realized that it was indeed the voice of Christ. Saul then became obedient and asked the Lord what he would have him to do. Saul began to pray to the Lord and, after receiving his sight, was filled with the Holy Ghost and was baptized. Saul began to spend time in fellowship with his disciples who were at Damascus. He preached Christ in the synagogues as a testimony that he is the Son of God.

Like Saul, as a new creature born again and filled with the Holy Ghost, your life should change. These changes may consist of places you go, people you spend time with, how you treat people, the way you dress, and your inward and outward appearance. Others should be able to see there is a difference in you as a change or a conversion. New creatures in Christ should not walk around grumpy, mad at the world, with a frown on their face and an unapproachable attitude. The way you carry yourself and the way you act should be a reflection of Christ. Others should look at you and want or desire what you have, which is a relationship with Christ.

"Then Peter said unto them, 'Repent, and be baptized every one of you in the name of Jesus Christ for the remission of sins, and ye shall receive the gift of the Holy Ghost (Holy Spirit)'" (Acts 2:38). When we receive Jesus Christ into our lives, we receive the baptism of the Holy Spirit. The Holy Spirit dwells within each Christian believer to guide us to live like Christ. He leads us to live holy and to do and say the right things. Our Christian walk begins when we receive the Holy Spirit into our lives.

We have to humble ourselves and repent for our sins, whether by omission or commission, those that we are aware of and those that we are not. Learn to pray and ask for his will and not your own. Many times when we pray, we want God to do what we want him to do and not what his will is for us in our lives and the lives of others. We can seek God's face and guidance by reading and studying his Word and should ultimately be willing to live and grow in Christ.

We should learn to be led by the Holy Spirit. Learn to keep silent before speaking and search for his words and thoughts. Always ask yourself, "What would Jesus do?" Before making a move, be sure you have sought out his advice and waited upon the Lord for an answer. This type of relationship does not happen overnight. It takes some time to learn and to know his voice. We have to learn to listen to his voice and his voice only. "But seek first the kingdom of God and His righteousness, and all these things shall be added to you" (Matthew 6:33).

When we grow in Christ, we should no longer desire to go to some of the places or events that we visited while in the world. As Christians, we are to be set apart from the rest of the world. It is not a sin to go to a club, for example; however, once you become saved and you desire to follow Christ and live according to his standard, you should no longer desire to go to some places as before. Our lives should start to mirror that of Christ.

When we grow in Christ, the way we dress should also change, and this includes our appearance when going to church. Many of us have heard the expression made by many churches, "Come as you are." This expression can refer to both your inside and outside appearance. We are, at this time, focusing on the outside. Once you have gained salvation and desire to follow Christ, our respect and responsibility to ourselves and those around us should change. We should love ourselves and others the way Christ loves us. Therefore, we should not want to cause disrespect to ourselves or cause others to be distracted or stumble and fall. We should have no desire to show our body to others outside or inside the church. You may feel that showing cleavage and thighs is very innocent, but unfortunately, it may cause a man to lust and not be focused on the Word.

You do not have to exploit your merchandise or advertise yourself as if you are on the trading block. The cleavage of a diamond shows an area where they are weak or unstable. What does showing your cleavage or your thighs say about you?

When you grow in Christ, others should see a difference in you. Like Saul, you should have a conversion. The things you used to do, you may no longer desire to do. God's light should shine around you and entice others to want what you now possess.

THE WORD

Acts 2:1-36 (The Gift of the Holy Spirit)

Acts 9:1-22 (Saul's Conversion)

Matthew 7:13-14

> Enter by the narrow gate; for wide is the gate and broad is the way that leads to destruction, and there are many who go in by it. Because narrow is the gate and difficult is the way which leads to life, and there are few who find it.

Luke 11:28

> But He said, "More than that, blessed are those who hear the word of God and keep it!"

Matthew 10:38-39

> And he who does not take his cross and follow after Me is not worthy of Me. He who finds his life will lose it, and he who loses his life for My sake will find it.

Matthew 5:16

> Let your light so shine before men, that they may see your good works and glorify your Father in heaven.

Matthew 16:24

> "If anyone desires to come after Me, let him deny himself, and take up his cross, and follow Me."

SISTA TO SISTA

Sista, whatever you do in your daily life, it should be a reflection of Christ's image. When you grow in Christ, you should have a new walk and new talk. Your actions, desires, and motives should be different because you now should want what Christ wants for your life. You are now being led by his will and not your own. You should be singing a new song and dancing to a different beat. Just waking up every morning should give you a reason to rejoice! Sing hallelujah!

DISCUSSION

_____

_____

_____

_____

_____

_____

_____

_____

_____

_____

_____

_____

_____

_____

_____

_____

_____

_____

_____

_____

_____

_____

_____

_____

_____

_____

_____

_____

_____

CHAPTER 4

Relationships

Blessed is the man who walks not in the counsel of the ungodly, Nor stands in the path of sinners, Nor sits in the seat of the scornful.

—Psalm 1:1

THERE ARE MANY DIFFERENT TYPES of relationships. A relationship can be a bond with family members, friends, coworkers, or church members, just to name a few. When we decide to live according to the Word of Christ, our relationships may change or require avoidance. There should be evidence of a visible or heartfelt difference in how a Christian relates to others in their environment, whether it is with a family member, coworker, friend, or just simply someone you encounter in the supermarket. As Christians, we are the light and not darkness, and therefore, that light should be evident in our daily walk.

When you choose to grow in Christ, you may encounter or feel a strain in certain relationships. The feeling of not fitting in or not desiring to participate in activities that was once enjoyable prior to your growth. The feeling of discontentment should become overwhelming as well as the urge to no longer be a part of "the crew." When you are growing in Christ, your light is no longer blending in with the darkness of past relationships. At this point one must learn to distance themselves from these relationships and desire to seek a different path—one called holy and righteous.

As Christians we should avoid lifestyles and relationships with the ungodly or unbelievers. We should be a witness to them and not allow ourselves to be sucked in or tainted by the choices they make. We are to remain holy in their presence and not allow ourselves to be persuaded or encouraged by their actions and behaviors. We are to affect them and not allow ourselves to be infected by these past relationships. Once we are strong and mature in our faith, it should not be as hard to remain holy among our past. But until that time, we may find that distance is the best alternative. That is not to say we don't love or support them or are no longer friends or family, but we can learn to love from a distance and give support and encouragement without our walk and relationship with Christ being affected.

People often say, "You become what you hang around." There is a lot of truth to this statement. Words and actions of those around you can cause harm or good to your life. When you are growing in Christ, choose to interact with people who inspire you to be the best person that you can be. Make sure that you are affecting others around you, and you are not allowing them to infect you.

We have to avoid approval of sin, or turning a deaf ear and a blind eye to opportunities to be a witness of righteousness; however, don't be judgmental. Remember, we were once in their shoes. We are blessed when we seek to live holy and obey God's will. We are the heirs to the eternal kingdom, sons and daughters of the King, and we are to carry ourselves in such a way that speaks royalty.

THE WORD

2 Corinthians 6:14-18

Do not be unequally yoked together with unbelievers. For what fellowship has righteousness with lawlessness? And what communion has light with darkness? And what accord has Christ with Belial? Or what part has a believer with an unbeliever? And what agreement has the temple of God with idols? For you are the temple of the living God. As God has said:

"I will dwell in them
And walk among them.
I will be their God,
And they shall be My people."

Therefore

"Come out from among them
And be separate, says the Lord.
Do not touch what is unclean,
And I will receive you."
"I will be a Father to you,
And you shall be My sons and daughters,
Says the Lord Almighty."

Proverbs 12:5

The thoughts of the righteous are right, But the counsels of the wicked are deceitful.

Proverbs 24:1-2

Do not be envious of men, Nor desire to be with them: For their heart devises violence, And their lips talk of troublemaking.

1 Corinthians 5:9-13

I wrote to you in my epistle not to keep company with sexually immoral people. Yet I certainly did not mean with the sexually immoral people of this world, or with the covetous, or extortioners, or idolaters, since then you would need to go out of the world. But now I have written to you not to keep company with anyone named a brother, who is sexually immoral, or covetous, or an idolater, or a reviler, or a drunkard, or an extortioner—not even to eat with such a person.

SISTA TO SISTA

Sista, simply put, you must break, avoid, or cut off bad relationships! Relationships that come between you and Christ, or relationships that causes you to give up your integrity and moral standards, must be avoided. Remember, light and darkness have nothing in common. Stop trying to fit in when God has set you apart. God said to come out from among them. Seek counsel from those that are following God's Word and living in the light.

Refrain from seeking advice from the ungodly. This type of influence causes damage to your relationship with Christ. As subtle as it may sound, this advice is not good and will lead you down the wrong path with consequences. Pray and ask the Lord for discernment of those around you. As you continue to grow in Christ, ask Him to put people in your path that will be good and favorable for your life and your daily walk. Remember, God loves you enough to give up his Son for you, and therefore, he will always want what is best for you.

DISCUSSION

CHAPTER 5

Dating

He who finds a wife finds a good thing, and obtains favor from the Lord.

—Proverbs 18:22

DATING IS A MAJOR AREA with tremendous struggle for Christian singles. The traditional days of dating and courtship are viewed as a thing of the past, old-fashioned and played out, as they say. Long gone are the days when a man was the suitor and wooer to the female. Gone are the days when chivalry was alive and in full effect, when the man opened the door for a lady and paid for dinner when he was interested in her companionship. Gone are the days when ladies were really a lady, and men were really men. Why? We no longer have these standards in our society today. Females are not being ladies, and therefore, there is no expectation for men to be the man. Women today are chasing men instead of allowing a man to find a "good thing" so that he may obtain the favor of the Lord.

In our society today, women are not setting the standard by which a man should treat them; nor is the man looking for a Proverbs 31 woman, one of noble character and worth more than rubies. Many are seeking instant feel-good satisfaction to only gratify the desires of the flesh. Many singles are choosing today, in the twenty-first century, to have sexual relationships with people they really don't know. They are continuously putting themselves in danger with their lives, whether it is the threat of sexually transmitted diseases, date rape, or unwanted pregnancies.

God's plan was created to avoid such situations—to wait upon the Lord, to submit oneself and he will give you the desires of your heart. However, singles are choosing to ignore the scriptural guide that he created and opting to follow a plan that is not pleasing to the Lord. The self-determined plan comes with complications, feelings of loneliness, inadequacy, desperation, and anxiety, emotional strain, divorce, self-destruction, poverty, increased number of children in single-parent homes, men jailed for nonpayment of child support, fatherless children, and the list goes on and on.

We must begin by once again setting standards. Ladies, if you give all the perks of marriage away or for free, why would a man feel an obligation for marriage? Why buy the software when you can download it free? If someone gives you a free cell phone with unlimited usage free of charge, why then would one choose to pay to enter into a contract and have to adhere to all the rules and regulations of the contract? Therefore, ladies, stop giving the perks of marriage away. You allow a man to move in with you or you move in with him without marriage, then you get mad and upset when he does not marry you.

Single women sometimes question why they are not finding a husband or prospering according to what the Word tells us. Many may fail to realize that maybe, just maybe, it is because they are not following his Word and the plan that he has provided. Failure to do his will, to follow his plan, and thinking that he does not see all that we do—we are merely fooling ourselves. Many of us have struggled or are still struggling with this concept.

In the fourth chapter of John, we find a Samaritan woman that came to the well to draw water. Jesus asked her for a drink of water. After verbalizing to the woman about the type of water that he could provide, with which she would never thirst again, he then told her to go call her husband and come back. She stated that she had no husband. Jesus called her out and told her of the five husbands that she had, and the one she was with now was not her husband. Jesus knew of her indiscretions and the life that she led. He knows all and sees all because he is God. Don't be fooled by the expression "What is done in the dark stays in the dark." God can and will bring situations to light.

The story of Ruth is one of the greatest love stories. After the death of Ruth's husband, she decided to accompany her mother-in-law, Naomi, to Bethlehem, where Ruth gleaned in a field owned by a man of good standing named Boaz. Boaz was quite smitten with Ruth upon first encounter, and after inquiring as to whom she belonged, Boaz made provision for Ruth by making sure she was protected in the field and would have enough grain to collect. As the story unfolds, Boaz was a gentleman and was one of Naomi's kinsman-redeemers who stepped up to the plate and married Ruth with the assurance of having deep love and respect for her.

In the story of Ruth, Ruth did not see this fine wealthy man in the field and go chasing after him. She did not seduce him and disrespect herself. She did not flaunt her breast and dangle her thighs. Instead, she followed the Israelite custom and lay at his feet at the threshing floor. She allowed Boaz to follow his custom and make sure he was legally eligible to marry her. This was all a part of God's plan.

Singles, if you are not waiting on God's direction and what he has for you, you may be interfering with genealogical links. Ruth's meeting with Boaz was not a chance meeting; it was God ordained. Their relationship was important in the genealogical link from David to Christ.

Stop searching for a mate and compromising the value that our heavenly Father has placed on your life. He wants to give you Goshen—the best of the land. You can't meet the right person that God has for you if you continue to stay in a relationship with the wrong person. God may be sitting back, saying, "She's not ready," or "She wants to hold on to table scraps when I am trying to give her prime rib." You have to be willing to let go of what is not good for your life in order to receive that which is good and favorable from the Lord. If you continue to think that what you have is good enough, then you will not strive to go beyond and achieve what is exceedingly above and beyond what you can possibly imagine. Patiently wait and allow God to send you your Boaz.

Social Media Dating

Social media dating has become very popular with modern technology. However, it can be very dangerous. Singles, when meeting through social media, remember there is no sure way to really know who is on the other end. Many sites are set up to allow you to enter your data about yourself. How many people do you think will lie? Gender, race, height, weight, residential location, age—all can be fabricated. Discretion and good old common sense should be used when venturing out to this form of dating. However, we often use the term *common sense* loosely, failing to realize that what may be common sense to some may not be common sense to others. Therefore, I have provided a list.

Common Sense List for Social Media Dating

- Never give personal information when you initially meet someone online.
- If you use a webcam, never have information on walls or on your desk that will identify your location or pictures of children or other identifiable objects in view.
- When deciding to meet, always decide on a public location, and it is a good idea to bring friends.
- Make sure you are not followed home when leaving.
- Never go to his home alone when initially meeting.
- Never leave your glass or food unattended.
- Ask personal questions and listen to the answer.
- Always follow your gut feeling.
- Never loan or give money or credit card information to an online date.
- If something does not feel right, don't hesitate to end the date.
- Do not share full names of close friends or relatives initially.
- Never send provocative pictures—they can be used against you.
- Always let someone know where you are going when meeting an online date.
- Never go out of town by yourself to visit someone you met online.

Dating with Children

When you are single with children and desiring to date, many circumstances must be considered. Children are not rag dolls, and you cannot drop them off and pick them up whenever you feel like it. They are your responsibility to raise—your first priority. Some of you may have to put dating on hold. We have to first consider the needs, well-being, and safety of our children as our first and utmost priority.

I have heard of a countless number of single parents who drop their kids off with anybody to babysit when they go out to clubs and parties. This is *not* safe! In today's society, morals, common sense, and respect have just gone down the drain. When you leave your children with any Tom, Dick, or Harry to babysit, you are opening the door for harm to come to them. Even some family members cannot be trusted with your children. Male or female children, it does not matter to pedophiles that are out there lurking and just waiting for the opportunity to defile your child.

Be smart about dating. Children should not see men coming in and out of your home. They should not have to wake up in the morning and see a man in the house whom they do not know. When you have a teenage girl, you must make sure your date is not there looking at her (or these days, your son).

Many ask the question, "When should I introduce my date [boyfriend, girlfriend, etc.] to my children?" The answer to this question may vary depending on who you ask. However, children should not meet someone you are dating unless you are getting serious about that person. With this said, once you have introduced them, listen to how your children feel about them. Older people say, "Children and animals can sense the true character of a person." So don't ignore your children when they express their opinion. If there are unresolved issues, never choose a man over your children.

Fornication

Remember, the body is the temple. If you are sleeping with a man and letting him violate your temple, you are missing out on your blessings by not living by the will of God. The Word tells us, "Marriage is honourable in all, and the bed undefiled: but whoremongers and adulterers, God will judge" (Hebrews 13:4 KJV). Do I need to explain this scripture? Let's see, not married, having sexual relations—whoremonger. God created sex to be enjoyed in marriage. So wait until marriage.

"Do you not know that the unrighteous will not inherit the kingdom of God? Do not be deceived. Neither fornicators, nor idolaters, nor adulterers, nor homosexuals, nor sodomites" (1 Corinthians 6:9). "And such were some of you. But you were washed, but you were sanctified, but you were justified in the name of the Lord Jesus and by the Spirit of our God" (1 Corinthians 6:11). Although in these scriptures Paul is describing unbelievers, when we as believers are seeking to grow in Christ, we should refrain from such behavior. Flee fornication. "Flee sexual immorality. Every sin that a man does is outside the body, but he who commits sexual immorality sins against his own body" (1 Corinthians 6:18). If you stumble and fall, repent and ask the Holy Spirit for strength in this area.

Types of Men to Avoid

- **The Noncommitting Man**
  This type of man will not commit to a relationship and certainly not marriage. This type of man usually has multiple women that he will usually engage in sexual intercourse. This man lacks judgment. Therefore, do not try to change him. He is showing

you his traits up front, and it is up to you to be smart enough or strong enough to avoid him. Beware! (Galatians 6:7-8, Proverbs 6:32)

- **The Married Man**
  Be careful not to fall for a relationship with a married man. This relationship is not of God. Usually this encounter will start with a married man engaging in conversation with a single woman. He may initially use her as a sounding board to listen to his issues with his home life. He may state that he is not happy with his wife and plan to leave her, trying to get the single woman to feel emotionally saddened for him. The next thing you know, you will find yourself in bed with him. Avoid this encounter. Refer him to another married man for counsel if he is looking for someone who can identify with his circumstance and offer him advice. (Hebrews 13:4, 4:13-27, Proverbs 6:20-35.) "Thou shalt not commit adultery" (Exodus 20:14).

- **The Maintenance Man**
  This is the man that a single woman will call for sexual pleasure. Avoid this type of man. He is only fulfilling flesh and destroying your relationship with God. (Proverbs 7:1-27.)

- **The Freeloader**
  This is the man that will ask you for money and wait on you to cook him a meal after you get off work. He usually lies around all day, asks to drive your car and drop you off where you need to go, moves in with you, and usually will not work. Avoid, avoid, avoid! Remember 2 Thessalonians 3:10, "For even when we

were with you, this we commanded you, that if any would not work, neither should he eat." Consider the story of the ant in Proverbs 6:6-11. The ant works hard carrying loads that are usually more than twice their size. They work diligently without a boss or leader to store up food for the future. If an ant knows the importance of working, what more should we expect from our men? It is important to earn your own bread.

- **The Mama's Boy**
  Sometimes a mama's boy is a good thing depending from what perspective we look at it. If a man loves his mother, has a close relationship with her, and treats her well, many times this may be foresight of how he will treat a woman, particularly his wife. However, sometimes this trait can backfire. Beware of the man who refuses to leave home or who runs to his mother every time he is in need of something. This type of man is not ready to grow up and take on adult responsibilities. If he cannot take care of and provide for himself, how can he be the head of the household and provide for you? (Ephesians 5:31-32.)

- **The Multiple-Baby Daddy**
  This type of man is similar to the noncommitting man. If this man has children from multiple women, he may have relationship issues, particularly with commitment. Run! Don't walk! Run! Not always, but usually, we see that this man does not provide for his children and is constantly in trouble with child support. What stability can this man provide for you?

- **The Dead-Beat Dad**

  This type of man will not provide for his children. If he refuses to provide for a child that he has already created, why would you desire to want a relationship with him and also risk having children with him? If you marry him, you will be caught up in child support with him and possibly be required to make his payments. Beware! First Timothy 5:8 clearly states, "But if any provide not for his own, and specially for those of his own house, he hath denied the faith, and is worse than an infidel."

- **The Abuser**

  This type of man will usually start the relationship showing no traits of abuse. He may then start being controlling, demanding, jealous, suspicious, and accusing. He will start subtle abuse—grabbing your arm or a push. Then he will tell you where you can and cannot go and who you can and cannot talk to or with whom you can or cannot have a relationship. This will escalate! Do not stick around to see the full escalation. He will continue to abuse. Why would you want a relationship with him? Don't say to yourself, "But he loves me," or "He will change." Not so without counseling. "Make no friendship with an angry man; and with a furious man thou shalt not go. Lest thou learn his ways, and get a snare to thy soul" (Proverbs 22:24-25).

- **The Unbelieving Man**

  This type of man does not believe in Christ and has no respect for Christianity. Do not be yoked with an unbeliever. "Be ye not unequally yoked together with unbelievers: for what fellowship hath righteousness with unrighteousness? And what communion hath light with darkness?" (2 Corinthians 6:14).

Types of Women, godly men Avoid

- **High Maintenance**
  This type of woman will usually require weekly hair and nail appointments. She will usually shop constantly to purchase the latest in fashion and every item of clothing must be name brand. If she can provide for herself that's not the problem. The issue with this type of woman is when she is looking for a man to provide this lifestyle for her.

- **Baby Mama Drama**
  This type of woman will constantly keep drama going with the father of her children. She is usually bitter and mad with him or with her situation. She cannot move on with her life because she is too consumed with making life miserable for him and those around her. She will usually try to keep the father from being a part of the children's life. He may have no desire for her or he fails to take care of his responsibility which is causing the bitterness.

- **Gold Digger**
  This type of woman is out to find a man that makes substantial income, regardless of his character. She will usually only date certain types of men, such as athletes, movie stars, lawyers, doctors or drug dealers. She looks at what he drives and the clothes that he wears to determine if she will even speak to

him. She is in search of a man that will take care of her financially with no regards to love, attraction or religion.

- **Round-the-Way Girl**
  This type of woman has had a significant amount of sexual partners. She may have low self esteem or trying to fill a void in her life. She makes poor choices in dating and is constantly looking for her next beau. She is looking for love in all the wrong places.

- **Trash Mouth or Cusser**
  This type of woman uses fowl language from sun up to sun down. She has little respect for herself or others around her that must listen to this type of language. She has no regard for who is listening, it does not matter to her. She does not realize how it makes her look. She may be beautiful on the outside, but when she opens that mouth it changes her whole appearance.

- **Know-It-All**
  This type of woman believes she knows all there is to know about any subject that comes up. This type of woman will argue until she proves her point. She may not accept the man being the head of the household because she believes that she knows what is best for any given situation.

- **Stalker**
  This type of woman will follow a man and spy on him to gather information or just because she wants to be with him. She may want to find out his routine or she has trust issues from past relationships. She will always

snoop; looking for evidence. You cannot leave your wallet or your cell phone unattended in her presence.

- **Controller**
  This type of woman wants to dominate over a man. She wants to be the head and make decisions for the relationship. She usually will not be submissive because she wants to be the big baller, the shot caller. She wants to make all the decisions as to where to go to dinner or a movie. She wants to dictate what a man should wear, how to think or what to say and even when to breathe.

- **Drunkard**
  This type of woman may enjoy the consumption of too much alcohol. She is usually in denial about her drinking. She will usually party and have a good time and not remember anything the next day. She may be drinking to avoid reality or she thinks that it is the only way to have a good time.

- **Provoker**
  This type of woman is always starting trouble and always in the middle of some type of drama. She is always in everybody's business and wants to confront people and start arguments. She is usually the one that is gossiping and carrying information from one group of people to another.

- **Drama Queen**
  This type of woman is always being dramatic. She must always be the center of attention and the loudest one in the room. She must be the center of

every conversation and require all eyes on her. Like the Provoker, she is always in everybody's business and wants to keep drama going. She is always seeking an audience.

- **Party Girl**
  This type of woman must be in attendance to everybody's event. She cannot miss a house party or dinner party because that is her life and her way of having a good time. She is usually not content or satisfied with being alone. She must always be in a crowd. She is usually the first to arrive and the last to leave any event for the sake of taking it all in and not missing a moment.

This information is not meant to be judgmental but informative. When we know better, we should strive to do better. These are a few of the traits in a woman that godly men run away from. The enemy is causing too many women to fall victim or prey to ungodly situations or relationships. It is the trick of Satan! Stop being a victim.

I remember so vividly the days my father taught the lesson, "Don't depend on a man." He would teach me how to check and change the oil in my car; how to change a tire; how to mow, aerate, and lime the grass; how to paint; and how to build a house board by board and brick by brick. I remember being right there soaking it all in. He would teach, "If you can do these things for yourself, then you will not have to depend on a man." Later in life, that lesson came more and more into the foreground of my daily life.

Gone are the days of chivalry when men did these things for women because that is just what a man is supposed to do. Now one would have to worry, especially single women, if these things are asked of a man, then we owe them something, other than money, in return, called gifts on demand.

There are many good, God-fearing men out there, but we have to watch for those who are not. We have to watch for those that will use opportunities when a woman is down to treat her as prey and use it for their gain. Some men may try to hit on a woman or make her feel obligated to give sexual favors in return for help in a situation, better known as gifts on demand.

Ladies, stop allowing yourselves to fall victim to this pitfall of the enemy. If you are dating and you begin allowing him to buy you material things, such as televisions, phones, cars, tires, furniture, paying your bills, or simply dinner, this opens the door for gifts on demand, meaning, "I give you something, and whenever I want sexual favors, then I expect them from you." This is how you get caught up and dependent. You will be forever indebted to him.

Therefore, ladies, be careful when you are seeking honest labor. Be careful when men offer to mow your grass or help with something around your home. Seek the Lord for discernment of his motives. Pray before you search and ask the Lord to send you a God-fearing, honest man when you are requiring a handyman for chores. Sometimes it's best to stick with the professionals even when we think we can't afford it rather than call Joe Blow, who is going to do the job and expect gifts on demand in return.

List of Dos When Dating

- Set your standards of how you want to be treated.
- Allow a man to be a man.

- Listen to what a man is telling you instead of trying to hear what you want him to say. If he tells you he does not want a relationship or to get married, that is exactly what he means. Stop thinking you are going to change his mind.
- Keep the drama out of dating.
- Stay steadfast with your morals.
- Have concrete conversations that allow you to discern his intentions.
- Ask open-ended questions (questions that require more than just a yes or no answer).

List of Don'ts When Dating

- Don't wear provocative clothing with your cleavage and thighs exposed—this sends a message, "Yes, I am open to having sex."
- Don't pay for meals (unless you decide to go Dutch—pay for your own) until you are far advanced into the dating stage, then you can offer. But don't allow him to make you think you are obligated to pay for a meal.
- Don't leave your glass unattended. Date-rape drugs are being used at an alarming rate. These drugs will cause sedation, and you will have no knowledge of being raped. Be aware!
- Don't equate a meal to sex. A meal does not equal sex—you are not obligated to have sexual intercourse just because a man pays for dinner. If this is his expectation, keep it moving and don't look back!
- Don't allow a man to leave his things around your home. He is marking his territory to ward off any other men.

- Don't "shack up," meaning living together before marriage.
- Don't fall for lies. Listen to your intuition, Don't play dumb.
- Don't play the "getting pregnant" game, thinking this will trap a man into marrying you—you will be a single mother raising a child by yourself.
- Don't discuss past failed relationships in the first stages of dating. Remember, get rid of all bitterness! You cannot move on to another relationship carrying baggage from past relationships.
- Don't be too quick to discuss where you work and what you do. Sometimes this is a way to determine how much you make.
- Don't date married men. A married man may tell you they are planning to leave their wife because they are not happy. Wake up! They are not leaving home! And surely you do not want to cause a failed marriage—this is adultery.
- Don't ignore the signs of abuse. When you first identify a trait of abuse in a date, run!

THE WORD

The Book of Ruth

John 4 (The Woman at the Well)

Hebrew 13:4

> Marriage is honorable among all, and the bed undefiled; but fornicators and adulterers God will judge.

Galatians 6:7-8

> Do not be deceived, God is not mocked; for whatever a man sows, that he will also reap. For he who sows to his flesh will of the flesh reap corruption, but he who sows to the Spirit will of the Spirit reap everlasting life.

Proverbs 6:20-35 (Beware of Adultery)

Proverbs 7:1-27 (The Crafty Harlot)

2 Thessalonians 3:10

> For even when we were with you, we commanded you this: If anyone will not work, neither shall he eat.

Ephesians 5:31-32

> "For this reason a man shall leave his father and mother and be joined to his wife, and the two shall become one flesh."

2 Corinthians 6:14

> Do not be unequally yoked together with unbelievers.

1 Corinthians 6:9

> Do you not know that the unrighteous will not inherit the kingdom of God? Do not be deceived.

Neither fornicators, nor idolaters, nor adulterers,
nor homosexuals, nor sodomites.

1 Corinthians 6:18

Flee sexual immorality. Every sin that a man does
is outside the body, but he who commits sexual
immorality sins against his own body.

SISTA TO SISTA

Sista, be careful when dating. Set your standards. Don't
compromise! This would be my top three on the list of advice
for dating. Never feel obligated to give in to flesh and worldly
expectations. As a Christian single, you are a child of Christ
and should walk in his image. Be in constant prayer for
deliverance from the weakness of your flesh.

Wake up and stop dreaming! Do you really believe that
the man you are shacking up with is going to just wake up one
morning and decide to marry you? Do you truly believe that
the married man you are sleeping with will one day decide to
really leave his wife? Do you hold on to the delusion that the
man who is showing his butt and underwear to the world will
miraculously one day have respect for you? My sista, wake up
and set your standards. A man will treat you according to how
you allow him to treat you. Love yourself and demand the
respect you deserve as a child of the King.

Remember, fornication is a sin resulting in pleasure that
only lasts for a very short period of time. It is not worth the
damage that it may cause. Sexually transmitted diseases
(including HIV, AIDS, herpes, etc.), unwanted pregnancies,
and guilt can be results of those few short minutes of pleasure
to the flesh. Weakness of the flesh is only a trick of the

enemy. His job is to kill, steal, and destroy you by any means necessary.

Take some of your focus off dating. Spend time working on your relationship with Christ. Study the Word and show yourself approved. Remember, your Boaz is being molded just for you. He will be worth the wait. Take the vow of purity from this day forward to wait until marriage. Allow the Holy Spirit to dwell within you and lead you to do what is pleasing to the Lord. Be saved, be single and be satisfied, my sista.

DISCUSSION

CHAPTER 6

The Role of Man versus the Role of Woman

And God said, "Let us make man in our image after our likeness: and let them have dominion over the fish of the sea, and over the fowl of the air, and over the cattle, and over all the earth, and over every creeping thing that creepeth upon the earth." So God created man in his own image, in the image of God created he him; male and female created he them.

—Genesis 1:26-27

In the beginning, God created man in his image and gave him specific orders—to have dominion over every living thing on earth. God decided it was not good for man to be alone, and therefore, he created woman from the rib of man. "And Adam said, 'This is now bone of my bones, and flesh of my flesh: she shall be called Woman, because she was taken out of Man.' Therefore shall a man leave his father and his mother, and shall cleave unto his wife: and they shall be one flesh" (Genesis 2:23-24). Then God gave them a charge to "be fruitful, and multiply" (Genesis 1:28).

Although in the same image, from the very beginning, men and women were created for specific tasks; man gave life to woman, and woman gave life to the world. Man was given the responsibility as the head of the family. Therefore, he had to be able to govern his own home, provide and protect, have dominion over his children, as well as the charge to teach and train his children in discipline and respect to love the Lord. The woman was to be a helpmeet, to birth the children, and to be submissive to her husband. According to Proverbs 31, she should be of noble character, having her husband's full confidence in her. She should bring him good and not harm. She will work long days to make sure her family is fed and speak with wisdom and faithful instruction.

Realizing that times have changed and some roles have shifted, we are still required as Christians to have some standards and expectations of our individual roles. Yes, many women are now opting to work outside the home, either forced by the economy or by choice, and some men are now electing to remain home with the children or just simply to remain at home. Whatever the choice and circumstances may be, we still have to use some discernment as to whether or not certain choices will be excepted when choosing a mate is concerned.

Here, again, certainly no judgments are being made, just merely observations and discernment as to whether or not God sent a particular individual to be your husband. For example, knowing that in the beginning God created woman to be man's helpmeet, if you as a woman choose not to be a helpmeet or you simply want to do things on your own, then why would you want to get married? If you do not want to compromise and always want things to go your way, then why get married? If you cannot accept that your husband will be the head of the household, then as a Christian woman, why are you contemplating marriage? You have a choice to remain single and be satisfied with your state of singleness.

Likewise, if a man does not want to leave his mother and father and cleave to his wife, then he should remain unmarried. If he cannot work (not including a man that has lost his job and looking for work), provide for his household, or be a role model for his future children, then he should remain single.

This is where we have to start using discernment, prayer, and that term that we use loosely, good old *common sense*. Ladies, if you have been in prayer for the Lord to send you your mate, then why would you think that he would send you someone that does not fit the biblical standards of the role of a man? Certainly, I am not suggesting that as a Christian single you must wait on a mate that is perfect. No, I am not reaching that far. I am merely suggesting that as a Christian single, have faith, pray, and wait upon the Lord to send you whom he has molded and perfected just for you. Don't compromise. Wait upon the Lord!

In Jeremiah 29:4-7, as a message from the Lord, Jeremiah instructed the Jewish captives of Babylon to build houses and settle down, plant gardens, and eat what they produce, then marry and have sons and daughters, find wives for their sons, and give their daughters in marriage so they too may have sons and daughters. They were also instructed to increase in number and seek peace and prosperity into the city to which they were carried into exile. Therefore, should Christian single women not expect a potential husband to be able to provide a roof over her head if he requests her hand in marriage? Can he figuratively grow a garden, meaning provide for her?

I have compiled a list of the roles of a man and the roles of a woman to help you. Certainly, these roles are not concrete due to life experiences, the economy, and the evolution of the world that we live in today. However, as Christian singles, there are still standards that one should expect when considering marriage or dating.

THE ROLES OF A MAN

- Saved, God-fearing, and filled with the Holy Spirit
- Provider
- Leader
- Good role model
- Trainer
- Communicator
- Protector
- Responsible
- Governor of his home
- Loving

THE ROLES OF A WOMAN

- Saved, God-fearing, and filled with the Holy Spirit
- Nurturer
- Caretaker
- Helpmeet
- Communicator
- Responsible
- Submissive
- Noble character
- Confident
- Loving

THE WORD

Genesis 2

Proverbs 31:10-31

The Virtuous Wife
Who can find a virtuous wife?
For her worth is far above rubies.
The heart of her husband safely trusts her;
So he will have no lack of gain.
She does him good and not evil
All the days of her life.
She seeks wool and flax,
And willingly works with her hands.
She is like the merchant ships,
She brings her food from afar.
She also rises while it is yet night,
And provides food for her household,
And a portion for her maidservants.
She considers a field and buys it;
From her profits she plants a vineyard.
She girds herself with strength,
And strengthens her arms.
She perceives that her merchandise is good,
And her lamp does not go out by night.
She stretches out her hands to the distaff,
And her hand holds the spindle.
She extends her hand to the poor,
Yes, she reaches out her hands to the needy.
She is not afraid of snow for her household,
For all her household is clothed with scarlet.
She makes tapestry for herself;

Her clothing is fine linen and purple.
Her husband is known in the gates,
When he sits among the elders of the land.
She makes linen garments and sells them,
And supplies sashes for the merchants.
Strength and honor are her clothing;
She shall rejoice in time to come.
She opens her mouth with wisdom,
And on her tongue is the law of kindness.
She watches over the ways of her household,
And does not eat the bread of idleness.
Her children rise up and call her blessed;
Her husband also, and he praises her:
"Many daughters have done well,
But you excel them all."
Charm is deceitful and beauty is passing,
But a woman who fears the Lord, she shall be praised.
Give her of the fruit of her hands,
And let her own works praise her in the gates.

Ephesians 6:4

And you, fathers, do not provoke your children to wrath, but bring them up in the training and admonition of the Lord.

Ephesians 5:22-33

Wives, submit to your own husbands, as to the Lord. For the husband is head of the wife, as also Christ is head of the church; and He is the Savior of the body. Therefore, just as the church is subject to Christ, so let the wives be to their own husbands in everything. Husbands, love your wives, just as Christ also loved the church and gave Himself for her, that He might sanctify and cleanse her with the washing of water by the word, that He might present her to Himself a glorious church, not having spot or wrinkle or any such thing, but that she should be holy and without blemish. So husbands ought to love their own wives as their own bodies; he who loves his wife loves himself. For no one ever hated his own flesh, but nourishes and cherishes it, just as the Lord does the church. For we are members of His body, of His flesh and of His bones. "For this reason a man shall leave his father and mother and be joined to his wife, and the two shall become one flesh." This is a great mystery, but I speak concerning Christ and the church. Nevertheless let each one of you in particular so love his own wife as himself, and let the wife see that she respects her husband.

SISTA TO SISTA

Sista, when discerning if a man is the one that the Lord has sent you, seek his guidance first and foremost. If the man you are considering dating or marrying does not possess the majority of the items in the list of the roles of a man, then he may not be the one. Likewise, do you possess the traits on the list of the roles of a woman? If not, you yourself may not be ready for marriage. Should a Christian single just ignore these traits and compromise for the sake of having a steady date or just to be married?

Vickie Blakeney Mitchell

DISCUSSION

CHAPTER 7

Are You Spiritually Ready for Marriage?

And the Lord God said, It is not good that the man should be alone; I will make him an help meet for him. Therefore shall a man leave his father and his mother, and shall cleave unto his wife: and they shall be one flesh.

—Genesis 2:18, 24

PAUL STATES CONCERNING MARRIAGE, "Now concerning the things whereof ye wrote unto me: It is good for a man not to touch a woman. Nevertheless, to avoid fornication, let every man have his own wife, and let every woman have her own husband" (1 Corinthians 7:1-2). However, he goes on to say, "But I say this as a concession, not as a commandment. For I wish that all men were even as I myself. But each one has his own gift from God, one in this manner and another in that. But I say to the unmarried and to the widows: It is good for them if they remain even as I am; but if they cannot exercise self-control, let them marry. For it is better to marry than to burn with passion" (1 Corinthians 7:6-9). Paul is saying that it is by God's grace that some remain unmarried and, therefore, able to concentrate completely on the work of the Lord. Some Christians have the gift of marriage while others the gift of being single. He believed that in the event that the unmarried and the widows cannot contain themselves, then it is best to marry and not burn from committing sexual sins against God.

There is more to marriage than just wanting to be married. It is more than just a ring, a pretty dress, and a wedding day. God created marriage for a man and a woman to be joined together in intimacy and sexual union. He placed man as head of the woman, as Christ is the head of the church. We should never enter into this union lightly, remembering why God created it and to show honor to him.

Are you a Proverbs 31 woman? Singles, as we read in Proverbs 31:10-31, we find the most inspiring example of a woman. She is a "virtuous woman," one with good morals and excellent character. It is almost impossible to be exactly like her as described, but we can learn from her qualities and character when determining if we are ready for marriage.

THE WORD

1 Corinthians 7:1-7

> Now regarding the questions you asked in your letter. Yes, it is good to abstain from sexual relations. But because there is so much sexual immorality, each man should have his own wife, and each woman should have her own husband. The husband should fulfill his wife's sexual needs, and the wife should fulfill her husband's needs. The wife gives authority over her body to her

husband, and the husband gives authority over his body to his wife. Do not deprive each other of sexual relations, unless you both agree to refrain from sexual intimacy for a limited time so you can give yourselves more completely to prayer. Afterward, you should come together again so that Satan won't be able to tempt you because of your lack of self-control. I say this as a concession, not as a command. But I wish everyone were single, just as I am. Yet each person has a special gift from God, of one kind or another.

Ephesians 6:31-33

As the Scriptures say, "A man leaves his father and mother and is joined to his wife, and the two are united into one." This is a great mystery, but it is an illustration of the way Christ and the church are one. So again I say, each man must love his wife as he loves himself, and the wife must respect her husband.

Mark 10:6-9

But "God made them male and female" from the beginning of creation. "This explains why a man leaves his father and mother and is joined to his wife, and the two are united into one." Since they are no longer two but one, let no one split apart what God has joined together.

SISTA TO SISTA

Sista, don't rush into marriage. If you are not ready to be submissive to a husband, to be a helpmeet to him, to bring good to him and not harm, to be loving, confident, and supportive to him, then you are not ready for marriage. If you cannot love God first and then yourself, if you cannot take care of yourself, take care of your own finances, be a caretaker (keeping a clean home and providing a meal), then you are not ready for marriage. Take this time to work on yourself. Build your relationship with Christ. If you have children, concentrate on their needs. When the Lord is ready, he will send you your husband, the one that is molded and perfected just for you. Prepare yourself and be ready! Until then, be saved, be single, and be satisfied.

DISCUSSION